WONDERFUL WORLD OF ANIMALS

© 1996 McRae Books

All rights reserved. No part of this book may be reproduced in any form without the prior written permission of the copyright owner.

This 1997 edition published by Brockhampton Press
20 Bloomsbury Street, London WC1B 3QA

Text by Beatrice MacLeod
Designed by Marco Nardi
Illustrated by Paola Holguín

Created and produced by McRae Books Srl
Via dei Rustici, 5 – Florence, Italy

ISBN 1-86019-584-9

WONDERFUL WORLD OF ANIMALS
BIRDS

Beatrice MacLeod
Illustrated by Paola Holguín

BROCKHAMPTON PRESS

WHAT IS A BIRD?

Birds come in all colours, shapes and sizes, from tiny bee hummingbirds no bigger than a man's thumb, to huge ostriches nearly three metres tall. However, all birds have four things in common: they lay eggs and they have beaks, feathers and wings (although not all of them can fly).

Ostriches are the largest birds in the world. They can't fly, but they can run very fast. Ostriches live in the savannas of Africa.

North African ostrich

Great blue heron

Herons have large strong wings. Their wings are covered with long contour feathers which help them glide effortlessly through the air.

Feathers

Birds are the only animals that have feathers. A bird's body is almost entirely covered in them. They protect it and keep it warm. Baby birds have fluffy, down feathers. As they grow, adult contour feathers appear, although they keep some down for warmth.

Where Birds Live

There are about 9,000 different species of birds. They live everywhere, from the poles to the equator. Each species is adapted to its environment. Penguins have thick skins with a layer of fat underneath to keep them warm, while eagles and albatrosses have powerful wings to glide and soar.

Bald eagle

Eagles live high up in the mountains. They build their nests on mountain crags, cliff tops or in the uppermost branches of tall trees. The bald eagle is the national bird of the United States. It lives along the coasts and around the rivers and lakes of North America.

Wandering albatross

Albatrosses spend almost all their lives gliding above the southern oceans. They soar on updrafts for hours at a time without flapping their wings. They only come ashore to breed.

Emperor penguin and chick

Penguins live along the cool southern coasts of Africa, Australia, New Zealand and South America. Only one species, the Galápagos penguin, lives in warm, tropical waters.

DIFFERENT HORIZONS

Some birds spend their whole lives in the same habitat, such as a forest or pond. Others migrate, often flying long distances to breed or to avoid harsh winter weather.

The **pintail** lives and nests in Europe, Asia and North America. It flies thousands of miles to the south in winter, in search of food and warm weather. The species is named after the the two long feathers in the male's tail.

Male pintail

Scarlet macaw

The **scarlet macaw** is just one of many brightly coloured parrots in the tropical forests of Central and South America. It has a long tail and splendid plumage in all the colours of the rainbow.

Parrots

Parrots sometimes live to ripe old ages (up to 80 years). Most can imitate the human voice. The African grey parrot is the noisiest.

Beaks and Food

Most birds use their beaks to catch and eat food. Because of this, a bird's beak often has a special feature or adaptation which helps it to get the food it most likes to eat.

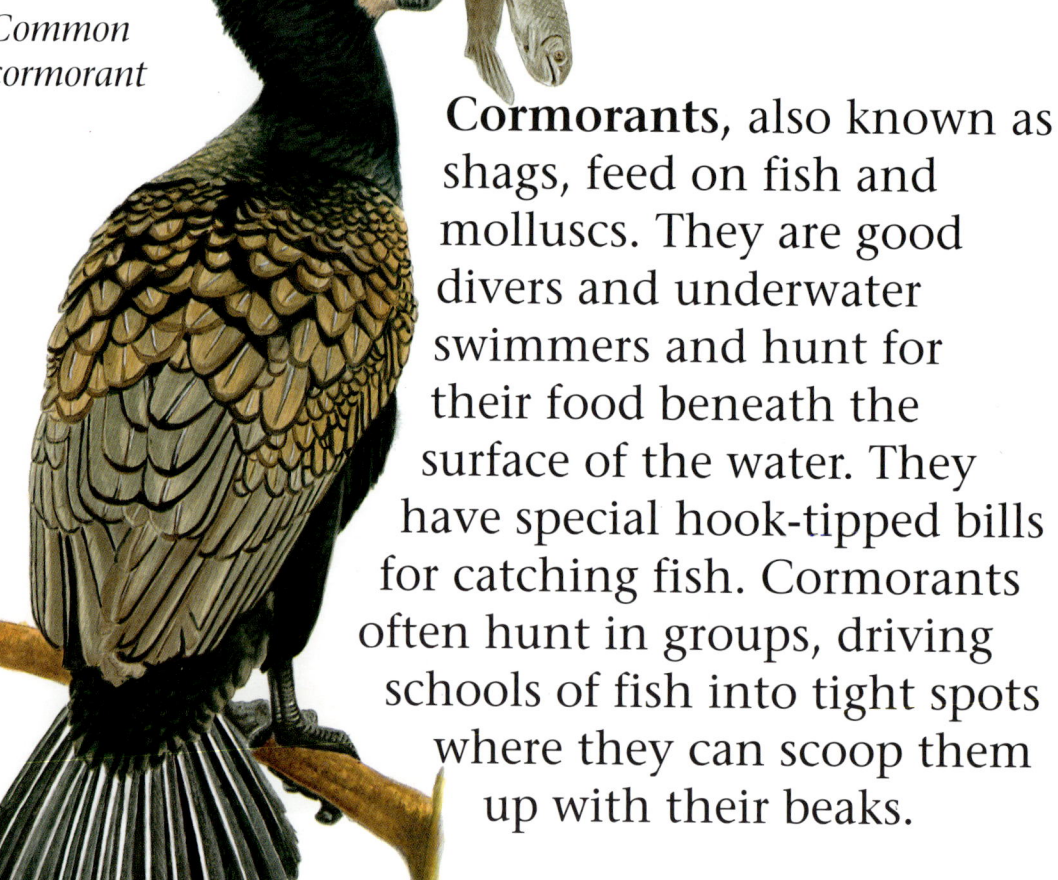

Common cormorant

Cormorants, also known as shags, feed on fish and molluscs. They are good divers and underwater swimmers and hunt for their food beneath the surface of the water. They have special hook-tipped bills for catching fish. Cormorants often hunt in groups, driving schools of fish into tight spots where they can scoop them up with their beaks.

Hummingbird

Hummingbirds like to eat nectar. They use their long beaks to reach inside flowers. Hovering in front of a flower, they beat their short wings very fast, as they suck nectar up through their tube-shaped tongues.

Domestic canary

Canaries eat seeds, small succulent leaves and fruit. They particularly like to eat figs. Yellow canaries are usually cage birds. Wild canaries are greenish-brown in colour.

Hunting

Many birds feed on insects and other invertebrates which they catch in flight, pry from bark, pick out of plants or dig from the ground. Birds of prey have tough hooked beaks and long sharp talons for gripping their prey.

There are about 100 different species of **starlings**. European starlings were introduced to America and Australia where they are now very common. Most starlings have long, pointed beaks which they use to dig up insect larvae.

European starling

Saw-whet owl

Most **owls** hunt at night. They catch a variety of animals, including insects, frogs, fish and small mammals. They carry their victims in their bills before swallowing them whole.

Nocturnal birds

Very few birds are active at night. Owls are successful nocturnal hunters because of their large, sensitive eyes and very keen hearing. They can locate and capture a small rodent in total darkness from the noise it makes as it scuttles across the woodland floor.

Domestic birds

Early humans hunted birds and gathered their eggs to eat. The first farmers domesticated a number of birds, including chickens, geese, ducks and pigeons.

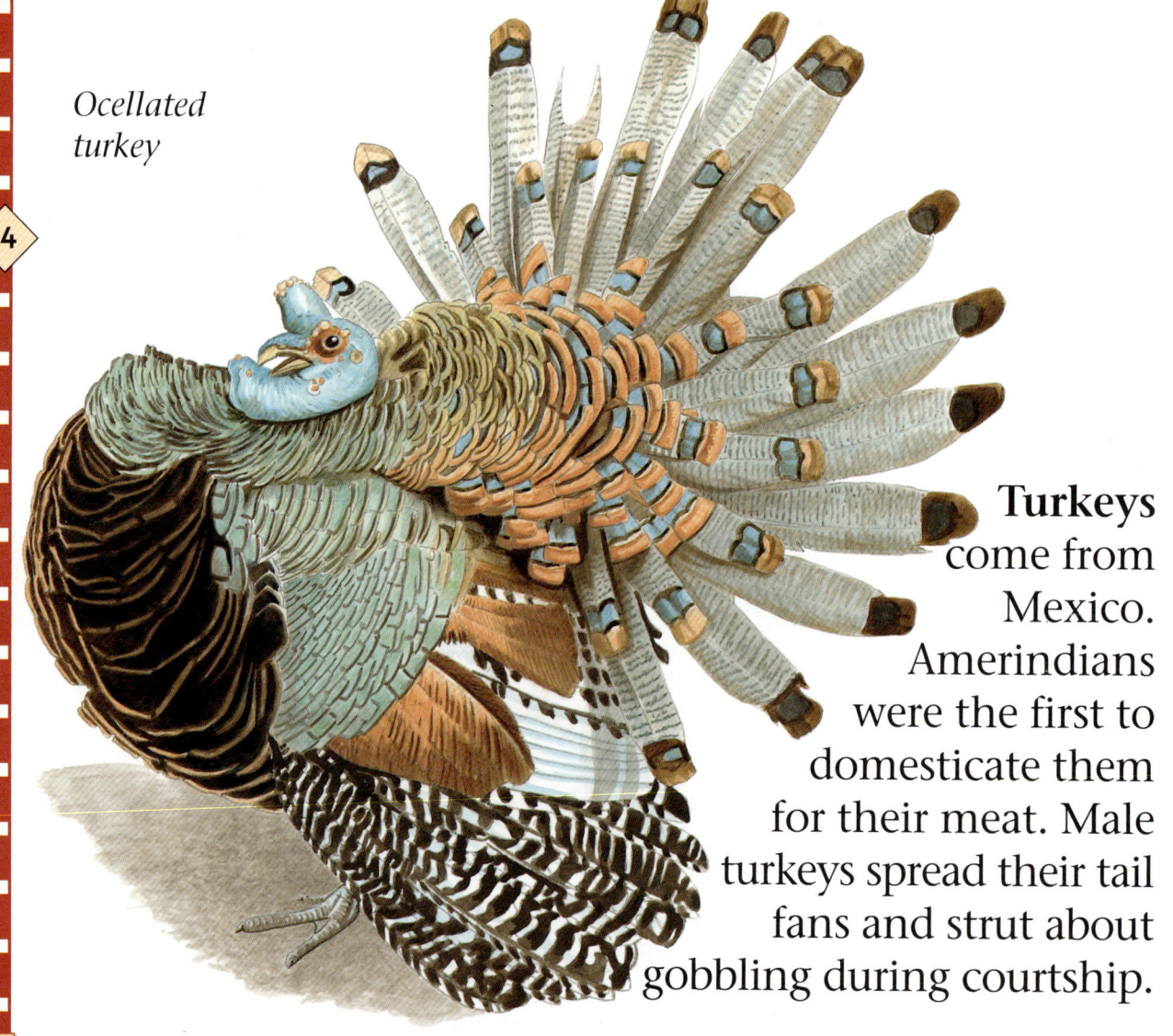

Ocellated turkey

Turkeys come from Mexico. Amerindians were the first to domesticate them for their meat. Male turkeys spread their tail fans and strut about gobbling during courtship.

Rooster

Chickens were tamed in Asia over 4,000 years ago. They were used for cockfighting rather than for food. Today, there are over 100 different varieties. They are kept for their eggs and meat.

Domestic goose

Geese are waterfowl. They are part of the same group as ducks and swans. The Ancient Egyptians kept geese nearly 4,000 years ago. Geese are a good source of meat, eggs, fat and feathers.

BLENDING IN

Birds are most at risk when they are resting, sitting on their nests or newly hatched. Chicks and fledglings often have drab feathers until they are old enough to fly and defend themselves.

Toco toucan

Blending in doesn't always mean being dull. Tropical rain forests are full of vivid green leaves, bright flowers, and richly coloured animals. **Toucans** have huge colourful beaks which may help keep them safe in their dazzling surroundings.

Some birds change colour from season to season. This **ptarmigan** is white in winter, white with a brown neck in spring, speckled brown in summer, and brown and white again in autumn. It changes its coat to blend in with the landscape so that hungry predators won't see it so easily.

Arctic ptarmigan

Bright and dull

Many birds have brightly coloured feathers. Males are often more colourful than females. Males use their showy plumage to attract a mate and to defend their territory. Females, who usually sit on the nest, need to be less visible or they will be caught and eaten.

Birds at Work

Birds have a lot to do. They must find enough to eat for themselves and their families, keep clean, build nests, lay eggs and bring up their young.

Kingfisher

Kingfishers perch or hover above the water until they spot a fish, then they plunge down and scoop it up in their bills. They sometimes have as many as seven chicks, each of which eats about fifteen fish every day. A large family is a lot of work!

Common flicker woodpecker

Woodpeckers peck holes in trees where they, and other birds after them, can nest and bring up young. They also peck insects out from under the bark.

Village weaverbird

Male **weaverbirds** build elaborately woven nests using stalks of grass. Females come to inspect and if the nest looks good they accept the male as their mate.

Nests and chicks

Most birds build nests to lay their eggs in. Nests can be woven of twigs, grass or other plant material, and lined with pebbles, mud, feathers or animal hair. The variety is endless. All birds incubate their eggs and feed their young for the first days or weeks of their lives.

Grebes build floating nests. When the young hatch their parents carry them on their backs.

Great crested grebe

The **cuckoo** lays its egg in the nest of another bird. When the young cuckoo hatches, it tosses the other eggs from the nest so that it can have its foster parents' undivided attention.

Cuckoo chick and warbler foster parent

Eggs

Birds' eggs vary enormously in shape, colour and size. The smallest egg, laid by a tiny hummingbird, is only about 1 centimetre long. On the other hand, an ostrich egg can weigh over 2 kilograms! Eggshells have tiny holes in them so that the baby bird inside can breathe.

INSTINCT AND LEARNING

Most bird activities are done by instinct. Feeding, preening and breeding are automatic. But some behaviour is learned by copying others. Parrots can repeat human speech, although they don't know what they are saying.

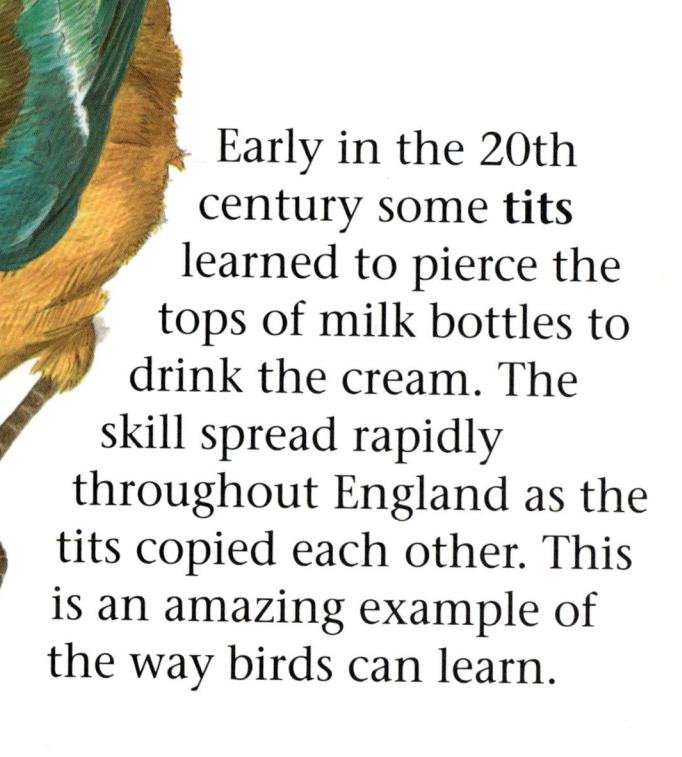

Blue tit

Early in the 20th century some **tits** learned to pierce the tops of milk bottles to drink the cream. The skill spread rapidly throughout England as the tits copied each other. This is an amazing example of the way birds can learn.

Herring gull and chick

Young **herring gulls** know that if they tap the red spot on their mother's beak she will regurgitate food. The chicks are not taught to do this, they know by instinct.

Songs and calls

Nearly all birds can 'sing', although they are not all musical. Birds sing and call to guard their territory, attract a mate or to warn each other of danger. Many birds can recognize their mate or young by their calls. Some birds can sing beautiful tunes.

Resting

Most birds can't see well at night. At sunset they go to special roosting places to sleep. Birds also rest during the day. When they are not feeding they take short naps. Some birds tuck their heads under their wings.

Canada geese

Canada geese breed in Alaska and Canada. They fly south to the USA and Mexico for the winter. During the long flight south the geese sometimes sleep as they fly.

Common swallow

In summer **swallows** build nests of mud and grass. The female swallow lays about four eggs. She sits on them for two weeks. When they hatch she is rested and ready to take care of the fledglings.

White stork

Like many wading birds, **storks** rest by standing on one foot. They don't like to untuck their legs and, if disturbed, will hop away rather than take them down.

The Strangest Birds

Some birds look strange because of the shape of their bodies or beaks or the colour of their feathers. When we look more closely, we often find that each of these features has a special purpose and helps the birds to survive.

American white pelican

Pelicans have very long beaks, sometimes measuring up to 50 centimetres in length! They feed exclusively on fish, which they capture using their inflatable throats like fishing nets.

The **condor**, the largest bird of prey in the world, lives in Patagonia and in the Andes Mountains. Like many birds of prey, it flies effortlessly, soaring on currents of hot air.

Condor

Puffin

Puffins live in the far north. They are ungainly looking birds. In spring their beaks turn many different colours.

INDEX

Albatross 7
American white pelican 26
Arctic ptarmigan 17
Bald eagle 6
Blue tit 22
Calls 23
Canada goose 24
Canary 11
Chicken 15
Common cormorant 10
Common flicker woodpecker 19
Condor 27
Cormorant 10
Cuckoo 21
Domestic goose 15
Duck 8
Eagle 6
Eggs 21
Emperor penguin 7

European starling 12
Feathers 17
Goose 15, 24
Great blue heron 5
Great crested grebe 20
Grebe 20
Gull 23
Heron 5
Herring gull 23
Hummingbird 11
Kingfisher 18
Macaw 9
Nocturnal birds 13
North African ostrich 4
Ocellated turkey 14
Ostrich 4
Owl 13
Pelican 26
Penguin 7

Pintail 8
Ptarmigan 17
Puffin 27
Rooster 15
Saw-whet owl 13
Scarlet macaw 9
Shag 10
Songs 23
Speech ability 5
Starling 12
Stork 25
Swallow 25
Toco toucan 16
Toucan 16
Tit 22
Turkey 14
Village weaverbird 19
Wandering albatross 7
Warbler 21
Weaverbird 19
White stork 25
Woodpecker 19